Breaking the Ice

306 Great Conversation Starters

Dave Sherman

Connection Pros

Breaking the Ice —306 Great Conversation Starters

ISBN: 0-9742504-6-5

Cover and Interior Design by The Printed Page, Phoenix, Arizona

Printed in the United States

Dedication

For many years, I've been approached by people who have confessed that the one thing that causes them the most pain and discomfort about meeting and connecting with others is not having any idea of what to say after they introduce themselves. Well, this book is dedicated to all of you who have shared your pain with me. Without all of you, this book probably would not have been written. I hope this book will start to make you feel more comfortable and confident when it comes to meeting people.

Introduction

Hi. My name is Dave Sherman. Thanks for taking a look at my latest book. For those of you who don't know me, I am a connections expert. What makes me a connections expert? I know exactly what it takes to create a connection between two complete strangers. How does one do this? Well, if I told you that, then you wouldn't have to purchase this book. Since I believe that you have to give before you can receive, allow me to share with you the secret of creating connections with others.

If you take the time to create a level of **likeability** and **commonality** with other people, you will find yourself making more connections than ever before. People build relationships with others that they like and that they know. How do you create this level of likeability and commonality? You need to start talking to people about the things that really matter to them and this book can help you do just that.

This book contains 306 of the best conversation starters I know. One of the biggest challenges people face when it comes to meeting and connecting with others is that they don't know how to strike up a good conversation. This book will help you to start conversations with just about anyone you meet. You can use it at networking functions, dinner parties, family reunions, singles events, and so many other places.

Who can benefit from *Breaking the Ice?*

▲ **Business people** – It's perfect for meeting and connecting with new people.

▲ **Singles** – It's just the thing you need to help you meet that special someone.

▲ **Families** – Use it when that annual get together is starting to get a bit dull.

▲ **Married couples** – When you're tired of talking about work, family, or money, this book will help.

▲ AND SO MANY MORE!!

Every good connection begins with a conversation. As simply as I can put this, *Breaking the Ice* will help make you feel more comfortable and confident when it comes to carrying on these conversations. The more comfortable you feel, the more times you'll want to start conversations, and the more opportunities you'll have to create meaningful connections with others.

I hope you enjoy my book and, as always, if you have any questions, comments, suggestions, or ideas for other conversation starters, please feel free to call me at 480-860-6100 or send me an e-mail at Dave@ConnectionPros.com.

Three Ways to Get the Most From This Book

1. Keep this book with you at all times. Buy a few copies and keep one in your car, your office, and your house. This way, you'll always have access to great conversation starters and you'll never feel uncomfortable when you meet someone new. Also, my wife, Randi, and kids, Lyndsi and Mathew, would really appreciate the extra sales.

2. Always follow up most answers by asking why. One of the best ways to learn about people is to ask why they answered the way they did. The more time someone takes to answer each question, the more information you will learn and the more new conversations will be generated.

3. Make sure you always listen to how they respond to your questions. People don't like to talk when they know that others aren't listening. People who exhibit good listening skills are considered smarter, friendlier, and much better looking. Okay, the better-looking part isn't true but the first two are definitely true. So, spend more time listening and watch how people start connecting to you!

1) Describe how you got into your current line of work.

2) Describe your business in 60 seconds or less.

3) Describe the best piece of advice you can offer from your industry.

4) Describe what you'd like your title to be for your current job.

5) Describe the greatest benefit your company can offer a prospective customer.

6) Describe your perfect client.

7)   Describe a great lead or job referral for you.

8)   Describe the types of industries on which you focus.

9)   Describe what you like most about your job.

10) Describe what you like
    least about your job.

11) Describe your greatest
    work achievement.

12) Describe your worst
    professional failure.

13) Describe your most
    embarrassing work moment.

14) Describe your educational
    background.

15) Describe your greatest
    professional challenge.

16) Describe your favorite business book.

17) Describe whom you would pick to be your ultimate business mentor.

18) Describe the person for whom you have the most respect in business.

19) Describe your greatest strength in business.

20) Describe your greatest weakness in business.

21) Describe why someone should be doing business with your company.

22) Describe the best piece of business advice you ever received.

23) Describe the best places you go to connect with other professionals.

24) Describe one thing you would change about your professional life.

25) Describe your very first job.

26) Describe the worst you job you've ever had.

27) Describe your favorite vacation spot.

28) To where have you traveled that you never want to return?

29) What is your favorite cocktail?

30) What is your biggest pet peeve?

31) Describe your greatest
guilty pleasure.

32) Who, living or dead, do you
truly idolize?

33) What three words best
describe you?

34) What would you like to have written on your tombstone?

35) What is your favorite spectator sport?

36) What is your favorite color?

37) What is your favorite food?

38) What is your favorite card game?

39) What is your favorite board game?

40) What was your favorite childhood game?

41) Describe your favorite game to play with your child/grandchild.

42) Describe your dream date.

43) Who would be your dream date?

44) Describe the best date you've ever been on.

45) Describe the worst date you've ever been on.

46) Describe your perfect mate.

47) Describe your perfect honeymoon.

48) Describe your perfect wedding.

49) What was your favorite childhood TV show?

50) What's been your favorite TV show as an adult?

51) What is your favorite movie?

52) What was the first movie you ever remember seeing?

53) Describe a movie that always makes you cry.

54) What's your favorite song?

55) Who's your favorite musical performer?

56) Who's your favorite actor/ actress?

57) Describe the kind of music you listen to regularly.

58) Have you ever met anyone famous?

59) What was your most unusual family experience?

60) What was the funniest wedding moment you've ever seen?

61) What was the worst
wedding moment you've
ever seen?

62) Describe your most
annoying habit.

63) Describe your most
embarrassing habit.

64) Describe your favorite foreign country.

65) When and where was the first time you ever traveled internationally?

66) What was the best advice given to you by your father?

67) What was the best advice given to you by your mother?

68) Describe the best piece of advice you learned from your kids.

69) Describe the best piece of advice you learned from your spouse.

70) What was your father's
favorite figure of speech?

71) What was your mother's
favorite figure of speech?

72) Describe a moment from
high school that you'd like
to go back and relive.

73) How have your looks changed since high school?

74) Describe your favorite high school teacher.

75) Describe the teacher that had the greatest impact on your life.

76) Describe your favorite class in high school/college.

77) Describe yourself when you were in the best shape of your life.

78) Describe your first love.

79) Describe your greatest athletic achievement.

80) Describe the time in your life when you were the happiest.

81) Describe your favorite part of your body.

82) Describe your least favorite part of your body.

83) Describe the actor/actress who would play you in a movie about your life.

84) Describe your perfect last meal.

85) Describe your favorite decadent dessert.

86) Describe your least favorite food.

87) Describe the best meal you've ever eaten.

88) Describe what you would add to create the perfect ice cream sundae.

89) Describe your favorite comic strip.

90) Describe a summer vacation from your youth.

91) Describe a time when you conquered one of your greatest fears.

92) Describe your favorite childhood book.

93) Describe your favorite book as an adult.

94) Describe your favorite comfort food.

95) Who is your favorite author?

96) Describe the most exciting thing you have EVER done.

97) Where are you in the birth order of your family?

98) Describe your unofficial "title" in your family.

99) What is your favorite brand of chewing gum?

100) Describe your favorite type of doughnut.

101) Describe your favorite type of chocolate candy.

102) Describe your favorite type of non-chocolate candy.

103) Describe your favorite childhood candy.

104) Describe the first law you would pass if you were president for a day.

105) Describe the first thing you would do if you were God for a day.

106) Describe how you would spend one million dollars in 24 hours.

107) Describe the first thing you would buy if you won the million-dollar lottery.

108) What is the one word that would best describe your driving?

109) What is one word that
would best describe your
personality?

110) Describe the longest
childhood road trip you
ever took with your family.

111) What was the first album
you ever purchased on CD?

112) What was the first movie you ever purchased on DVD?

113) Describe the first time you ever drank too much.

114) Describe the worst weather you have ever experienced.

115) Describe the first time you ever lived away from home.

116) What sports did you play as a child?

117) What sports do you play as an adult?

118) How did you come up with your current e-mail address?

119) Describe the first time you ever broke the law.

120) Describe what you would do to undo a time when you really hurt someone close to you.

121) Describe the most expensive piece of clothing you ever bought.

122) Describe where you would live if you could live anywhere in the world.

123) Describe your dream home.

124) Describe the most extra-
vagant purchase you've ever
made.

125) Describe your favorite
piece of clothing.

126) Describe your very best
childhood friend.

127) Describe your very best
friend as an adult.

128) Describe a food you've
tried but will never eat
again.

129) Describe some of the
magazines to which you
subscribe.

130) Describe one food you refuse to eat.

131) Describe a type of music to which you refuse to listen.

132) Describe the first disease you would cure if you could.

133) Describe the political office for which you would like to run.

134) Describe your personality.

135) Describe your greatest high school experience.

136) Describe your extra curricular activities from any of your school days.

137) Describe your favorite holiday movie.

138) Describe your favorite romantic movie.

139) Describe your favorite
action movie.

140) Describe your favorite meal
at a Chinese restaurant.

141) Describe the toppings you
like on your pizza.

142) Describe your favorite childhood breakfast cereal.

143) Describe the type of fruit you like to include in a fruit salad.

144) Describe your favorite summer fruit.

145) Describe your favorite kind of pie.

146) Describe your favorite flavor of ice cream.

147) Describe the type of music your parents listened to when you were a kid.

148) What is your favorite number?

149) Describe any vices you currently have in your life.

150) Describe what you miss most about being a child.

151) Describe what you fear most about growing old.

152) Describe the house in which you grew up.

153) Describe the kind of grades you got during any of your school years.

154) Describe the type of "group" you hung out with most in high school.

155) Describe the person after whom you were named.

156) Describe how you came up with the names of your kids.

157) Describe your first family pet.

158) Describe your current family pet.

159) Describe the most unusual pet you've ever owned.

160) Describe your first experience with the death of a pet.

161) After whom were your kids named?

162) Describe any hidden talents that you might have of which most people are unaware.

163) Describe the first words ever said by your kids.

164) Describe some of the habits you do at home but would never do anywhere else.

165) Describe the comfort clothes you change into after a day of work.

166) Whom *do* your kids most
look like?

167) Describe your favorite TV
show theme song.

168) Describe your favorite
childhood snack food.

169) Describe your favorite movie sequel.

170) Describe your favorite soft drink.

171) Describe the most memorable professional sports moment you ever witnessed.

172) Describe the first planet you would like to visit.

173) Describe your first car.

174) Describe the thing that frightens you most.

175) Describe three people, living or dead, that you would like to have join you for a dinner for four.

176) Describe one deceased member of your family with whom you would like to have one more conversation.

177) Describe one thing you'd like to change about your current living quarters.

178) Describe one area in which you would like to be an expert.

179) Describe any celebrities that you might look like.

180) Describe what you would say if you had the chance to meet the President of the United States today.

181) Describe the amount of money you would like to receive so you would never have to work again.

182) Describe your all-time favorite restaurant.

183) Describe your most memorable birthday.

184) Describe which supernatural powers you would like to possess.

185) Out of your five senses, which one would you most hate to lose?

186) Describe the company of which you would like to be CEO for a day.

187) Describe the store at which you'd shop if everything was free for one day.

188) Name the song that best describes you and your life.

189) Describe how you would like to spend the very last day of your life.

190) Describe how you would like to be remembered.

191) Describe the one person you would call if you needed to be bailed out of jail.

192) Describe the first question you would ask if you met God today.

193) Describe the charity that would be the recipient of all of your money.

194) Describe one event that you would like to go back in time and prevent from happening.

195) Describe the method of execution you would have to choose to end your life.

196) Describe the title of the book that could be written about your life.

197) Describe one fictional character to whom you'd like to be married.

198) Describe your favorite amusement park ride.

199) Describe one law that you would like to never have to obey.

200) Describe one crime that you would like to commit if you knew you would never be caught.

201) Describe the first thing you would do if you suddenly found out that you were invisible.

202) Describe which fictional parents are most like your own.

203) Describe your favorite time of year.

204) Describe the country you would like to own.

205) Describe the best idea
    that you have ever had.

206) Describe the worst idea
    that you have ever had.

207) Describe the one product
    that you wish you had
    invented.

208) Describe one product that you wish had never been invented.

209) Describe the qualities that you feel constitute a great boss.

210) Describe the qualities that you feel constitute a great parent.

211) Describe one of the saddest moments of your life.

212) Describe one of the happiest moments of your life.

213) Describe one of your personality traits that you would like to pass on to your children.

214) Describe what you would do to help end world hunger.

215) Describe one country that you would like to eliminate.

216) Describe the one thing you would offer passengers to make airplane travel more enjoyable.

217) Describe the one thing you would like to see offered at hotels to make your stay more comfortable.

218) Describe one gadget/option that you wish was offered on automobiles today.

219) Describe the one modern convenience you could not live without.

220) Describe your favorite
electronic gadget/device/
toy.

221) Describe how you would
make airline travel easier.

222) Describe what you feel is
the most stupid sport of
all time.

223) Describe a sport that you
would like to see added to
the summer/winter Olympics.

224) Describe a sport that you
would like to see eliminated
from the summer/winter
Olympics.

225) Describe the one cable
channel you couldn't live
without.

226) Describe your perfect secretary or professional assistant.

227) Describe the musical instrument you've always wanted to learn how to play.

228) Describe one person you wish you had never met.

229) Describe the actor with
    whom you would like to do a
    love scene.

230) Describe one person that
    you would like to help
    without him/her knowing
    about it.

231) Describe the one crisis in
    the world that you would
    like to eliminate.

232) Describe how much money you would need to call yourself rich.

233) Describe what courses you would take if you were to return to college.

234) Describe the musical group for which you would like to be the lead singer.

235) Describe one person that you would like to bring back from the dead.

236) Describe what you would do for work if you no longer needed money.

237) Describe the first group of people that you would help if you were to win the lottery.

238) Describe one heredity trait that you don't want to pass on to your children.

239) Describe one natural disaster that you would like to witness.

240) Describe the tourist site that you would most like to see in the USA.

241) Describe the tourist site that you would most like to see outside of the USA.

242) How many foreign counties have you visited?

243) How many states have you visited?

244) Describe your favorite
      thing at the circus.

245) Describe what you like
      most about going to the
      zoo.

246) Describe the first time you
      ever saw the ocean.

247) Describe one time when you thought you cheated death.

248) Describe the things that make you most happy.

249) Describe the things that make you most sad.

250) Describe your favorite type of weather.

251) Describe a historical event that you would have liked to witness.

252) Describe one historical event in which you would have liked to have been a participant.

253) Describe one thing that
     you like about the future,
     as compared to the past.

254) Describe one thing that
     you like about the past, as
     compared to the present.

255) Describe the greatest
     thing ever invented.

256) Describe your favorite flavor of birthday cake.

257) Describe the first funeral you ever attended.

258) Describe the greatest item that has ever been passed down to you.

259) Describe how you have most
impacted the world around
you.

260) Describe your worst
experience at the dentist.

261) Describe some of the
smells that always remind
you of home.

262) Describe some of your favorite smells.

263) Describe some of your favorite sounds.

264) Describe the position in which you typically sleep.

265) Describe one big-time award that you would have liked to have won.

266) Describe some of the childhood games you used to play.

267) Describe how you load a new roll of toilet paper on the holder.

268) Describe your favorite flower.

269) Describe your favorite flavor of bagel.

270) Describe how you take your coffee.

271) Describe how you squeeze a tube of toothpaste.

272) Describe the sports team you would like to own.

273) Describe the sports team you would like to manage.

274) What would you name a
     town that was being
     named after you?

275) Describe the charity that
     is the recipient of most of
     your funds.

276) Describe the part of your
     body you would like to have
     pierced.

277) Describe the part of your body you would like to have tattooed and what would that tattoo be?

278) Describe your favorite childhood possession.

279) Describe the time that you were most embarrassed by one of your siblings.

280) Describe the time that you were most embarrassed by your parents.

281) Describe the best joke that you have ever heard.

282) Describe the oldest joke you know.

283) Describe the most beautiful place you have ever visited.

284) Describe where you are originally from and how long you've lived where you currently live.

285) Describe how you ended up living in the place in which you currently are living.

286) Describe what you like to
do when you're not working.

287) Describe your dream
vacation.

288) Describe something about
yourself that most people
don't know.

289) Describe the proudest moment of your life.

290) Describe the most embarrassing moment of your life.

291) Describe your favorite holiday tradition.

292) Describe an event in your life that you would like to go back in time and experience again.

293) Describe your greatest childhood memory.

294) Describe one physical feature that you would like to change about yourself.

295) Describe your favorite hobby.

296) Describe your family.

297) Describe who you would like to be reincarnated as, living or dead.

298) Describe your earliest childhood memory.

299) Describe your greatest fear in life.

300) Describe what makes you most memorable.

301) Describe your "perfect" day.

302) Describe what you would
    like your obituary to say.

303) Describe some of the
    nicknames you've been
    called in your life.

304) Describe one wish that you would like to come true today.

305) Describe the time in your life when you were having the most fun.

306) Describe a conversation starter that has worked for you. After you've had a great conversation about your conversation starter, please send it to Dave for his next book. Dave's e-mail address is Dave@ConnectionPros.com

About the Author

Dave Sherman, "the connections expert," has been helping people all over the country create deep, powerful, and productive connections with others that have helped them personally and professionally.

As the founder and creator of "Connection Pros," a speaking, training, and consulting organization, Dave inspires people to look at the process of creating connections in a whole new light that is more effective, more comfortable, and more profitable. His topics include "Success is Just a Handshake Away," "Turning Casual Contacts into Potential Prospects," "Creating Connection Without Saying A Word," and more. Dave is also the author of the best selling book, *50 TOP TIPS, A Simple Guide to Networking Success*, as well as numerous other CD and video programs.

Dave has had the pleasure of working with Wells Fargo, Southwest Airlines, Merrill Lynch, Smith Barney, American Express, Northwestern Mutual, Medtronic, and over a dozen Chambers of Commerce all over the country.

Dave, married to Randi since 1988 and father to Lyndsi and Mathew, lives in beautiful Scottsdale, AZ. He loves golf, international travel, action movies, and his only real vices these days are a glass of Chardonnay and a good Cuban cigar.

For more information about Dave, please go to www.ConnectionPros.com or call him at 480-860-6100.

Order lots of copies of *Breaking the Ice — 306 Great Conversation Starters* for your friends, family and business associates.

❏   YES, I want·_____ copies of *Breaking the Ice — 306 Great Conversation Starters* at $12.95 each, plus $4.95 S&H (throughout the U. S.)

❏   YES, I want to receive my FREE subscription to *Connection Central e-zine*. My email address is listed below.

❏   YES, I am interested in having Dave speak to my organization. Please contact me with details.

My check or money order for $ _____ is enclosed. Please make your check payable to Connection Pros

Please charge my: ❏ Visa ❏ MasterCard ❏ American Express

Credit card # _____
Expiration date (month/year)_____ / _____
Three digit Security code (from back of card)_____
Name_____
Organization_____
Address _____
City_____State _____Zip_____
Phone_____Fax_____
Email (please print clearly)_____
Signature _____

Return to: Connection Pros
                   10128 N. 119th Place
                   Scottsdale, AZ 85259
                   Telephone Orders: 480-860-6100
                   Fax Orders: 480-451-9484
                   Internet Orders: www.ConnectionPros.com